Two Lives

Me in 1965

Two Lives

by
Andrew Cooper

Paradise Press

First published in Great Britain in 2017 by
Paradise Press, BM Box 5700, London WC1N 3XX.
www.paradisepress.org.uk

Copyright © Andrew Cooper 2017.

Andrew Cooper has asserted his moral right to be
identified as the author of this work in accordance
with the Copyrights, Designs and Patents Act 1988.

All rights reserved. No part of this publication may be
reproduced, stored in a retrieval system, or
transmitted, in any form or by any means, electronic,
mechanical, photocopying, recording or otherwise,
without the prior permission of the copyright owner.

A CIP catalogue record for this book
is available from the British Library.

ISBN 978-1-904585-88-6

10 9 8 7 6 5 4 3 2 1

Printed and bound by Print2Demand Ltd, Hastings.

Cover image by Dorian Aroyo.

Designed and typeset by Ross Burgess.

Set in Century Schoolbook, with
headings in Happy Monkey.

For Dorian

Acknowledgments

THANKS to the members of the Gay Authors Workshop for their help and guidance, and especially to Jeremy Kingston for his time and advice without which I would have been floundering badly, and to my publisher, Ross Burgess, whose comments and meticulous editing have been invaluable. And, of course, to Donald West who had no idea the journey he would send me on when we chatted over a cup of tea.

Contents

Prologue	1
Red Nails	2
Fairies and Other stories	5
School	6
It Can Happen	11
Music and Dancing	13
Moving House – Again	16
New School	18
Romantic Entanglements	24
Further Conflict	27
London Here I Come	32
St Stephen – Patron Saint of Typists	35
Rush of Guilt	37
Partners	39
Continuing Conflicts	44
Developing Circles	46
Give it a Try	49
Freud and Me	50
Jung and Me	54
Open University	55
This is It	56
Permission Granted	59
Last Job and Retirement	61
Just Friends	63
Revelation	64
Epilogue	67

Illustrations

Frontispiece:
  Me in 1965

Between pages 38 and 39:

1. Girls together?
2. Anne, Janet and me
3. Dad, Mum and me
4. Janet – with plaits! and Anne
5. Me – without plaits, but with my new tricycle
6. Jolly hockey sticks!
7. Man changes into Woman (from the *News Chronicle*)
8. Liz on holiday with me and my family with a wasp up her skirt! Early 1960s
9. Liz putting on a brave face having slipped on seaweed – Mum in the background struggling
10. Betty and me in *The White Horse Inn* – mid-1960s
11. Caroline and Liz
12. Hill School – with Scripture Union badge – 1951
13. Aldy (Alderson) and me in a photo booth
14. Aerial view of Ottershaw School
15. Day out from school – Dad and me punting
16. Chris, my best friend from school, and me in Bath having just left school
17. Christmas on H Ward (where I 'saw' Mr Hayward) – me, the Charge Nurse and John.
18. In the Staff Restaurant with chums – me far right at the back
19. Getting my Bronze Medal, 1965
20. Is this the right image for London …?
21. … or is this better?
22. Typing an OU assessment
23. Off to a Scottish Ball
24. Trixie, me, Gill and Ian
25. Proudly showing off my handwork, my prize-winning cardigan, my beard and my perm
26. Psychology degree from the OU
27. Me, Dorian and Roger Baker – author, gay campaigner, and friend of Dorian's – 1983
28. Ken Livingstone's Partnership Registration – me and Dorian
29. Married at last!

Prologue

IF I HAD KNOWN THEN what I know now, I wonder how different things would have been. Certainly I would have had a lot less unhappiness and confusion. Yet I might not have met so many interesting people. The Journey might have been quieter, but far less fascinating. I wouldn't have learnt so much about myself, and, by extension, other people.

We all have 'ifs' in our lives. If my mother hadn't suffered the anguish of a stillbirth a couple of years before I was born; if people hadn't been afraid to understand what they were seeing; if we were all brave enough to take a plunge into strange territory, what a different account this would be.

With all the developments in understanding human gender and identity I can't help thinking I might have ended up being a very different person – outwardly unrecognisable, but the same 'me' inside.

For much of my life I was intrigued by things spiritual, and initially subscribed to the Christian belief that 'you only live once', but dispensed with formal religions during my twenties. My journey to point of believing in reincarnation was a long, slow and, at times, sceptical one. Yet it is that journey, leading to belief, which finally sorted out my difficulties.

Red Nails

'MUMMY, will you buy me some red nail polish?'

'No, dear, I don't think so.'

'Oh pleeeeeeze!'

'No, darling,' in the 'don't ask again' tone that I realised made further requests futile.

A curious request for a young boy of four in the mid-1940s to make of his mother, although to me at the time it seemed reasonable enough. Let me explain.

Even at that age I knew that I was a girl. Overlooking a few rather crucial design faults, I should have thought it obvious to anyone of the meanest intelligence. After all, I enjoyed girls' toys, girls' games, knitting and being 'like Mum'. I was fascinated by knitting, and it must have been a godsend to Mum as it kept me quiet for hours on end. The result may not have been terribly successful – a bit tight and rather stringy. However, all my toys had lovely hot water bottle covers and scarves! That early introduction to knitting has enabled me, in later life, to knit any garment to the exact size specified in the pattern with the evenness of machine quality knitting, producing many garments for myself, friends and family. I even once won a local knitting competition. My elder half-sister, Anne, never really featured in my life as she was sixteen years older than me and left home to get married when I was seven. However, it was Anne who taught me to cast off knitting properly, for which I am continually grateful.

It did seem rather unfair that everybody was so slow to cotton on. After all, I was quite grown up now, and at four and a half I felt it was time I wore red nail varnish. Somehow people would have to be made to realise who I was. Even at that tender, and yet advanced, age I was not without a certain stubborn resourcefulness. I crept up to my bedroom, rooted around for my coloured pencils and *voilà*. Half an hour later – red nails. Not glistening and shiny, but still a start. My mother's joy was scarcely as unbounded as mine, particularly when it was discovered that the colour would not wash off. I was thrilled.

'Now what will the neighbours and the other children think?'

Strangely, I couldn't have cared less what the neighbours thought, and the other children couldn't have cared less what I chose to do with myself.

Bath time and energetic scrubbing to remove my 'nail polish' – to no avail. Then the usual request:

'Stand up, darling, and let me wash your body.'

This I discovered much later was my mother's delicate euphemism for my penis, but for a long time I referred to it as 'my body'. Only later did I name it 'my pissel'.

When not exploring various possibilities of homemade cosmetics, I used to be allowed to go across the road to play with some of the other local children. I clearly remember playing in the paddling pool and thinking what fun it was with the other girls, playing with their dolls and giggling. It could have been quite idyllic had it not been for those 'nasty, rough boys' who were a bit of a pain, the majority of whom thought I was a bit weird. Can't think why!

One of them must have taken a bit of a shine to me because we wound up in our garden shed one day and he showed me his 'body'. I was petrified. At the time I thought his 'body' looked all sore, red and raw. With hindsight I realise he must have had a foreskin and retracted it. Since I was circumcised (as was my father) I had never seen anything like this before and was thoroughly discombobulated. Although I arrived in the kitchen in mild hysterics, I never told my mother exactly what had happened. Was this the beginning of my secret exploration of male genitals – not my own? I wonder how the other child – also an Andrew – coped. A bit unnerving for him to discover that his 'body' could reduce someone to a gibbering heap in a matter of seconds – or perhaps not!

Fairies and Other stories

BEDTIME STORIES were wonderful and Mummy read them beautifully. I was enthralled and transported to many fictional worlds.

My absolute favourite book was *Dulcibella and the Fairies*. Although I couldn't yet read, it was full of the most lovely pictures of Dulcibella and loads of gorgeous fairies. Mummy used to read it to me, and the best bit was when Dulcibella was granted her wish to be a fairy for a day – my ambition, too. A long floaty, chiffony dress and huge wings – heaven!

I also loved the classic fairy stories. Goldilocks – so me, with long, blonde hair in plaits and that combined with perfect porridge. Who needs more? In later life I discovered that 'bears' has quite a different meaning and three is never quite enough! Cinderella – glass shoes, my favourite dancing and instant transformation into a beautiful girl. Somehow I still seem to find myself doing housework – but not, thank goodness, in the cinders! Not so keen on Sleeping Beauty – loved the lipstick in the illustrations, but a wicked stepmother and poisoned apples? Enough to put one off fresh fruit for life!

School

'WON'T IT BE FUN to go to school. A proper little boy in his uniform.' Not totally sure that I wanted to be a proper little boy, although I was dying to learn to read. And smart new clothes. Yes please.

I loathed my first school – in fact I wasn't too keen on most of them. I didn't understand what was going on. The girl next to me drew a super picture of a window with a flower in a pot in it. Somebody else knew how to add up and was praised for this. I just didn't fit in. I spent a lot of the time asking to go to the loo (outside in the playground) in the hopes that Mum would be coming just around the corner ready to relieve me from this misery. I thought she was being rather cruel inflicting this school on me, but later when I was grown up I discovered that she was just as agonised when she walked away hearing me wailing 'Mum, take me home.'

The boys expected me to join in with their football or games with guns – too rough – and the girls were unsure about a little boy joining in with their games, even though I loved playing with dolls and was a very gentle child. The boys thought I was a lost cause, but the girls were very generous.

Having wept non-stop for a week all the way to school because I couldn't bear it and all the way home with relief because I had survived, I was put down into a more junior class. Salvation was there in the form of a lovely teacher with long dark hair and a gentle voice. I thought she was the answer to a prayer, and I decided there and then to grow my hair long and have plaits. Coiffure in all its forms became the next point of disagreement after the cosmetic crisis of the red nails. I never wanted to have my hair cut. A compromise was arrived at and I was allowed to wear a plastic hairslide even in the street sometimes. Sadly, I have never achieved the ambition to have plaits and now I have only just about enough hair to cover my head!

Janet, my other half-sister who is nine years older than me, was given a new bicycle and I was given a new tricycle. For some reason, I always fancied myself riding a bicycle, then falling off it with my leg trapped underneath the front wheel and being rescued. Years of introspection leave me no nearer having a clue as to the meaning and fascination of this fantasy. I think I must have seen an illustration of this in a book. As far as I know Janet never fell off her bike. I always wanted to 'be like Janet' which I think nearly drove her mad at times.

The War had been over for about five years or so and we moved house from South London to the country – Old Oxted in Surrey. Janet started at a new school and was allowed to grow plaits; I started in a new school and wasn't. Oh well, at least I was sent to a mixed school where there would be other girls. I loved break time. In the nice weather, we would go out into the huge garden and I and the other girls would stand under the trees and giggle and sometimes we would hang upside down by our legs from the lower branches of the trees. I was so envious that the other girls had to tuck their gym-slips into their knickers. I longed to wear a gym-slip. So boring wearing trousers.

At times I was told 'Andrew, go over there and play with the boys.' I didn't want to play with the boys, and they didn't want an obvious cissy in their gang. It wasn't long before I oozed back into the girls' group and the teachers gave up badgering me.

Nasty old football reared its ugly head and to my horror I was expected to play it with enthusiasm. Mrs Hardy-Smith – who had hot breath and tried to teach me sums – took us for football. Apart from the fact that I was practically crippled by my agonising football boots, I didn't want to learn to play football. Those were the days when football boots had leather studs attached to the sole of the boot by three little nails. As soon as the studs started to wear down, the nails from the studs pushed through the sole of the boot and stuck into the soles of my feet. This was quite apart from the fact that the leather the boots were made of was so hard I could hardly hobble, let alone run after a ball and kick it. Dad, bless him, took pity on me and removed the evil studs and replaced them with rubber ones. Getting the old studs out was easy. Knocking little tacks through the rubber studs without a last inside the boots to make a rigid sole made hammering all bouncy. Truly this was a nightmare job for him. But with a certain amount of *sotto voce* swearing he made a marvellous job of it. This didn't improve my football or my handstands, but did eliminate the pain in my feet! There was only one thing for it, diversionary activity. I took myself off to the touchline as far away from the game as possible and practised handstands. Mrs H-S was not pleased, but seemed unable to stop me. The only problem was the evil football boots which upset my balance once they were waving about above my head.

On one occasion when my mother came to the school (can't think why) Mrs Hardy-Smith was heard to say 'Mrs Cooper, you know he should have been a girl.'

Too right Mrs H-S. You may have got unbelievably hot breath but you never spoke a truer word. Mum didn't really know what to say. I remember almost saying 'Can I, please?'

When the girls did dancing in the gym, I was deliberately naughty and was sent to stand in the corner from where I had a perfect view of the dancing. I longed to join them, and the headmistress Miss Pace who played the piano for them. We all believed Miss Pace (who I thought was called Paste) wore a wig. Looking back, I think she probably did. She was very nice.

Hockey or lacrosse would have been more my scene, like the girls in the Angela Brazil books I loved reading at home. Phrases like 'Draw, Flavia, draw' uttered by enthusiastic chums on the touchline I found thrilling. In fact, some years later (after another house move) our neighbour, Linda, did play lacrosse at school and had a lacrosse stick. We quite often used to play with this, throwing the ball to each other to catch it in the lacrosse stick. I had never felt more 'Angela Brazil' in my life! Later, at my prep school, we did play hockey. I quite liked this, to my surprise. I think having a weapon with which to beat off other players was a huge help. However, this added confidence didn't enable me to hit the ball with any real conviction.

Perhaps I wasn't making enough effort. Nobody apart from Mrs H-S had really the remotest idea what was going on and who I thought I was. I decided this had to be tackled head on.

'Mum, if I think about it really hard just before I go to sleep will I wake up in the morning and be a girl?'

'Most unlikely, darling.'

'Unlikely' but not necessarily 'impossible'. Super. There's hope yet.

In an effort to add weight to my argument I decided to increase the pressure further. Family lunch on Sunday seemed to offer a good opportunity. Unusually, I had to leave the table and go for a pee. On returning to the dining room I said to my mother:

'Guess what.'

'Hmm, hmm?'

'I have to sit down to pee now.'

'I see. Finish your lunch.'

Once more unconvinced. It really was too depressing.

I needed to do something to make me feel like a boy, and cease wanting to be a girl. I dreamt up a magical scheme whereby if I somehow engineered a situation in which I could make my penis touch my father's then I would immediately become a boy and my current problems would no longer exist. Needless to say, it didn't happen – either the touching or the transformation – but for many years I think the magic idea persisted in the form of getting to grips (literally) with as many penises as I could. That, of course, hasn't worked either.

But – guess what?

It Can Happen

I DISCOVERED the most amazing thing. An article in the newspaper we had delivered every day at home told the story of how a man had turned into a woman. I'd never been wildly keen on the business/political pages of the *News Chronicle*, and I have no idea what possessed me to browse through it on this particular day. There it was. In print. Easy to read and the most wonderful and sensational thing I had ever seen. Robert Cowell had turned into Roberta Cowell with pictures to prove it. Long blonde hair, red fingernails, pouty red lips – everything I'd always dreamed of. I cut the article out of the paper in secret using Mum's nail scissors and pasted it into my own personal notebook as a sort of lucky talisman. I still have the article today in my memorabilia box and have a sentimental moment when I look at it even now. Even his/her birth certificate was changed.

I wondered how long I'd have to wait before it happened to me. He'd liked doing boys' things and had to wait till he had grown up before he changed. I'd liked doing only girls' things so I'd expect not to have to wait so long. I hugged my secret knowledge to myself and it made the taunts and teasing I got at school for being such a cissy miles easier to bear. I'd wondered if I'd have to be transferred to my sister's school. What would I have been called. Andrea? Rosemary?

I also thought that I might develop the 'feminine' side of myself a little bit more. Nothing excessive because of the boys at school, but a little bit.

Fingernails seemed a good place to start as Mum thought it important to have nicely cut fingernails, and above all *clean* nails. Perfect – until one of the teachers, Mrs H-S again, commented that it was inappropriate for a little boy to keep his clothes so clean and have such clean nails. I thought 'too bad,' and Mum said 'Rubbish.'

Interestingly all my animal toys – horses, dogs and rabbits – were male, whilst all my 'human' shaped toys such as a doll, purloined from my sister, my golliwog and my teddy – also a hand-me-down from my sister – were female. They had to have dresses and plaits and girls' names. I don't remember which was which now, but Mary and Jane were my teddy and golly. Teddy would have been more appropriately named Edwina, but I hadn't heard of that name yet.

I have always been fascinated by 'tarty' women. One day going home on the bus from the shops, which was unusual in itself as we generally had to walk, I saw the epitome of 'my sort of woman' on the bus. She was wearing lots of make-up, had red nails and loads of jangly jewellery and was eating crisps from a packet. Eating in public on a bus? Forbidden in my world.

'Don't stare, darling. It's rude.'

I continued to stare. I just couldn't believe that it might be possible to be like that. It was as if the picture of Roberta Cowell in the newspaper had materialised in front of me.

When I next watched Mum putting on her face, which I did very frequently, I chanted 'More, more,' as she put on lipstick. Which she did – and then proceeded to blot most of it off again.

Music and Dancing

I HAVE ALWAYS LOVED MUSIC, and started learning the piano very early. Both Mum and Janet played the piano and I couldn't wait to be able to do so, too. Miss Edwards bicycled to our house every week for my piano lesson, which was a real treat. Miss Edwards was tall and thin and sort of spiky. Her writing on my music was thin and spiky, too. She was an absolute dear and so kind to me. Apparently I had always responded to music by twirling and whirling round the room, and finally I negotiated with my parents that if I gave up my piano lessons I could have ballet lessons.

My best friend, Jane, who was beautiful and had plaits, did ballet and I wanted to be like her. On one occasion I went to watch her ballet class. Green with envy I watched combinations of *pliés*, *tendus* and *jetés*.

So – Bye, bye Miss Edwards and Hallo Miss Burton. Each week Mum and I trekked off to Redhill to Miss Burton's ballet school. I adored going to ballet, although I was terribly disappointed that Miss Burton didn't wear a tutu and pointe shoes. Instead she wore a pencil skirt and dangerously high-heeled shoes – not that I didn't love high heels, it just didn't seem right for a ballerina. Never mind. As soon as the pianist struck up the little boy dressed in swimming trunks (weird!) vanished and was replaced by an enchanting creature, a mixture of Jane and Dulcibella, whose dream of becoming a ballerina came closer with every *tendu* and *jeté* that was performed.

I never got round to practising the *pliés*, *glissés* and *ports de bras* that Miss Burton set me to do at home, but I did work tirelessly at standing on full pointe. I padded my soft-toed ballet shoes with rags and teetered round the house on pointe for as long as I could stand the pain. When I could finally walk the length of the kitchen on pointe, I went down there one morning while my father was eating his breakfast to show him what I could do.

I thought I was sensational. He didn't. Perhaps it was because I had gone the whole hog and worn the scarlet gypsy skirt from the dressing up box that put him off. I also wore the wool wig that Mum had made me, since she wouldn't buy me a proper hair wig.

Poor Dad. It's difficult to imagine what he thought he had spawned. I took his response to be indifference, but in fact I suspect he was utterly bewildered and didn't know what to say.

To my absolute envy, Jane had progressed enough in her ballet classes to be allowed to do proper pointe work in real pointe shoes. I remember watching her do this in class. I nearly dissolved with envy and delight. She was so generous and let me have turns in her pointe shoes sometimes – at home, of course. Pity they were black, though. I couldn't understand why Nick, my other friend who lived near Jane and me, didn't want to have a turn, too. He didn't want to wear the dresses and fabulous false plaits that Jane had for dressing up either. We decided to settle for him being the boy and me being the girl. Jane in her gentleness masterminded our games.

A few years later Mum found an advert for

ballroom dancing lessons for older children, to take place in the long school summer holidays. I was enrolled and every week I bicycled down to the Congregational Church Hall in Oxted, which was down the hill from where we lived. Hildora Mac was both exotic and an excellent teacher. I took to ballroom dancing like a duck to water. My main partner was Lesley who was tall and as enthusiastic as I. She was the only child of seriously wealthy parents and lived in the very select part of Hurst Green, near Oxted. Her parents bought a spare ticket for *My Fair Lady* just in case Lesley had a friend whom she wanted to take with her. Lucky me. I was the chosen friend. Chauffeur-driven to London. I enjoyed a light supper in the limousine, centre stalls and my introduction to Julie Andrews and musical theatre. Wonderful!

Lesley's mother got a nasty cold and couldn't go out, so Mum rang her and offered to do any shopping for her.

'How sweet of you, but I always have something sent down from Fortnum's.' Right! How the other half live!

My friend, Liz, also liked ballroom dancing and we spent many happy hours at the Orchid Ballroom in Purley.

I also danced in the local operatic and dramatic society productions.

Moving House - Again

WE SEEMED to be moving house endlessly, but in fact it was only the third or fourth time in my life. We moved to Hurst Green, way out in the country, about five minutes from Aunt Sally's house. What a treasure I found in my new friend, Liz – who remains a close friend today. She lived next door to my aunt Sally, and one afternoon when my family were visiting boredom set in. Neither of my two cousins, Simon and Anthony – the latter was to have a significant influence in my life – was at home and I was at something of a loose end. Sally suggested I see if Liz was in her garden next door. She was. So I crawled through the hedge and said 'Can I play with you?' We've remained friends ever since. Very early on we agreed that Liz was rather a boyish girl and I was rather a girlish boy so we met somewhere in the middle. More knickers-tucking into gym-slips by Liz and more envy by me saw us endlessly practising handstands, cartwheels and backbends. Careers in a travelling circus seemed our obvious choice at the time. Having married rather unhappily with three children, Liz is now happily married to Caroline, a delightful minister in the Church of England.

We were both keen readers and swapped books endlessly. The extra bonus for me was that Liz had a schoolgirl's comic every week called *School Friend*. This she passed on to me once she had read it, and I devoured it, identifying with all the characters. Even now I can have a little personal wry smile about 'Lettice Leafe', the Greenest Girl in the School.

My belief in a magical change into a woman was wearing thin and was further reduced when Liz started to produce breasts and I didn't. However, I was not to be put off quite that easily. Back to the bedroom again, this time armed with a ball of string and a pile of clean handkerchiefs. Deeply engrossed as I was in creating my boobs, I didn't hear my mother enter the room. There was no way I could pretend I was 'doing nothing', sitting there wearing my string and handkerchief B cups for all the world to see.

Now I'm for it, I thought. But no. My window of opportunity was being left open for me.

'Darling, you're too young for that yet. Put them away and come downstairs for lunch.'

I wonder why nobody ever asked me 'Why? What's wrong with being a boy?'

New School

CURIOUSLY ENOUGH I quite enjoyed my time at the Hill School. I had got there by way of Hillsbrow School which I loathed. The most disturbing thing at Hillsbrow was a senior boy who had enormously long legs, wore short trousers (God knows why) and had terrifically shiny shoes. He looked just like the then current advertisement for Cherry Blossom shoe polish, giving a shine 'two feet deep'. I was absolutely fascinated. I was equally fascinated by the games master who took us for swimming. He 'disappeared' into the woods to change after swimming (we had an outdoor pool) and I caught a glimpse of his impressive, uncircumcised penis. Intriguing. Filed away for future investigation.

The most lasting legacy from the Hill School is my flair for languages. I truly think that we learnt enough Latin to pass GCE by the time we were twelve. We did an hour and a quarter of Latin *every* morning with Basher, as we nicknamed the Latin master. He used to roar at us, puce in the face and frothing with rage, if we made a mistake when standing in line to translate Caesar or parse sentences. We all shook in our shoes, but, my goodness, we got good at Latin. For some reason, Basher rather liked me and spent a certain amount of time stroking my hair and on one occasion wrote a long poem about it which began 'By fairy hands in moonlight pale 'tis spun.' I suppose now he would be hauled up for inappropriate behaviour, but it did me no harm, in fact I really liked him.

Miss Bowie took us for French and English. For some reason she spat all over everything when she spoke. If she came over to my desk to check what I was doing and made a comment on my work, this resulted in that page of my exercise book being covered in tiny droplets of spit.

Miss Bowie decided to put on a couple of scenes she had adapted from *Alice in Wonderland* – the ones where Alice meets the Fish and Frog footmen before going into the Duchess's house. To my delight she chose me to play Alice. At last I would get to wear a wig with long hair. But no, alas. Just a skirt and top. Yet another teacher who almost realised who I was.

To this day, I cannot imagine what possessed me to choose to go to boarding school, particularly as I had been offered a place at Whitgift School (where my heroine Roberta Cowell had gone). In some curious way I thought that I needed to leave home in order to try and sort myself out. I thought it might be like *Six Sinners at St Swithuns* or *Bunty of the Lower Fourth*. It wasn't and it didn't really sort me out. Ottershaw School was a direct grant public school and in fact gave its pupils a very good all-round education.

About this time I had to face the fact that I was very frightened of men. As a child I had been afraid of 'nasty rough boys' and as I grew up it became 90 per cent of men. These were other people's fathers, bus conductors, gangs of workmen, all of whom I thought would twig that I wasn't a proper boy/man. Some men who were gentler and had something 'other', made me feel much safer. Although at that time I didn't know anything at all about homosexuality, I wonder if some of them may have been gay.

Liz had just changed to a new all-girls school and that would really have suited me perfectly. As it was I had to contend with masses of boys hell-bent on 'taking it out' on anybody who didn't fit the mould. Me. The majority of the boys were real oiks (in my teenage opinion) and I was ragged rotten because I spoke 'proper'. I was called Lulu with oblique reference to the song 'Lulu had a baby and named him sonny Jim. She put him in the bath tub to see if he could swim.' Heaven knows what the perceived relevance to me was. I hated this nickname at the time, although now I would love it.

Once again I found myself desperately homesick and bawling my eyes out in the basement loos whenever I had a letter from home. Nothing was done properly at school and the idea of 'comfort' was a complete anathema to the powers that be. Lumpy porridge, cold fried eggs, endlessly feeling hungry. How we ever grew up into adults I'll never know, and some of the boys were total men by the age of 15. Nobody seemed to realise that I would have been better off at Roedean! – where I gathered from Lesley they had lumpy custard. Lumpy food is obviously a feature of boarding schools.

The nice thing was that Ottershaw introduced me to the notion of homosexuality. I enjoyed the many and varied sexual contacts I had with older boys at school. I loved playing with their cocks – particularly if uncircumcised – and making them come. I also enjoyed them bringing me off, but this was always of secondary importance to making sure they had a good orgasm. The only anxiety in all this was fearing being found out by the staff, but we had our secret places – in the props store under the stage for one. I think the slight element of danger was an added spice – as indeed it was subsequently in my cottaging days. I remember Nobby Clarke liked to wind the tab curtains at the side of the stage around both of us while we stood facing each other. He was the nearest experience I had to 'making love' as he enjoyed stroking legs and balls and having this done to him, rather than a hasty wank.

I think it may have been about this time that I thought it might be a lot easier to be a straight woman rather than (in those days) a criminal gay man. Conflict began to set in. I just liked looking after men – and being impressed by some people's considerable endowment. Also I was rather enjoying the pleasure my cock could give others and me.

At this point I think the seeds of a dual self were sown – the gay male Andrew, and the straight female Andrea. This was perhaps not unlike the condition of multiple personality except that I (Andrew) could choose which one I felt more like being.

At one level I felt thrilled that once again somehow people knew, unconsciously, who I really was, and gave me the name Lulu. The teasing and cruel jibes – not so good.

'Lulu, do you shave your legs?' this from 'Doy' Baker who had the reddest, poutiest lips of anyone, but wasn't queer (as we called it then) and had very hairy legs.

'No' (despite never growing hair on my legs).

'Are you a girl, then?'

Boys in the sixth form were allowed to take ballroom dancing lessons with a lovely young woman who came in to teach us. Needless to say, I enrolled immediately. The evening for the dancing lesson arrived and we all assembled in the big hall. I made a beeline for the teacher at one point and danced a quickstep with her. Thanks to the lessons with Hildora Mac I was able to lead her into a fishtail (which at that point she hadn't taught us). We performed it perfectly and she realised that I knew how to dance. From then on she put me to dance woman with some of the other boys. Geoff and Malcolm were two of the tallest boys and coincidentally very handsome men, so I was more than happy to dance as their woman. I don't know if they were overjoyed, but I loved it.

Some of the boys seemed to quite like my girlishness and even the Latin master had an affectionate name for me – Poppy. I was very good at Latin. I obviously had some sort of affinity and attraction for Latin masters. Could it have been the after-effects of a previous Roman incarnation?

As well as the sex, I enjoyed my time at Ottershaw once I got over leaving home. I loved learning – particularly languages and biology. And curiously, I've always quite enjoyed exams. Well – I liked showing off in my good subjects like Latin and French but I cringed in shame in the bad subjects. I once got a miserable 2 per cent for geography and was told I had to give it up if I promised to pass history which I was rather hopeless at, too.

Mum had a magazine called *Woman* delivered every week. In the school holidays she was frequently the last to get to see it. The letterbox crashed, and I pounced! Articles on fashion and make-up were my target and it was acknowledged that I knew more about what to wear with what, correct colour of eye shadow according to skin type and colouring, and how to put on lipstick without it smudging, than the whole of the rest of the family put together.

Slimming was also discussed at length, too, and so I decided that slimming was another way to try to show who I felt I really was. Mum was heard to say 'You're more fussy than a woman,' and Janet thought it was ridiculous, particularly as I was already slim. The result of this was a mild eating disorder in my thirties which has threatened ever since, despite now eating normally. The thinking isn't so normal, though.

Romantic Entanglements

BY THE TIME I WAS SEVENTEEN I knew for sure that I was the odd one out. Whilst other boys were discussing girls, I was inconveniently going weak at the knees at the sight of the PT master, and the day he actually steadied my legs whilst I was doing a headstand practically unnerved me for the rest of the day.

In the interests of being fair, Dad bought me a red BSA Bantam motorbike. He had done this for Janet when she was seventeen and did the same for me. It was so generous of him at a time when money was really short (when wasn't it?) and it took a lot of effort on my part to seem delighted. It was just too butch for me. I had mixed feelings about riding it because I got so cold. However, it was very useful later on.

Janet was no less than saintly as she taught me to ride it. (Dad by this time was very ill with multiple lung conditions that eventually killed him). In the space of a chilly afternoon on one of the quietest lanes near home, Janet taught me to ride. I have to say, I did feel rather triumphant.

Perhaps I just needed to fall in love with a woman. Christine was my new piano teacher for my last year at Ottershaw. An excellent teacher, enthusiastic and, sadly, unrealistic at least as far as I was concerned. She thought I was marvellous. I wasn't. I was good, but not nearly good enough to make a career as a pianist. Curiously, although I enjoyed her company, I felt less male with her than I did with the boys at school. Perhaps trying to fall in love with a woman was going to be the way to feeling better about myself.

She was only three years my senior and undertook to fall in love with me, or so she said. I spent time at her home with her parents and sister who were so welcoming to me as Christine's boyfriend. I knew Christine wanted more from me than I was able to give, for example when we kissed and she opened her mouth in a desperate attempt to induce intimacy. I remember I thought 'If only this was the PT master.'

I practised diligently and learned enough to pass Grade 8 with distinction, playing Bach, Beethoven and Chopin and later bringing the house down at the Parents' Day concert with the Chopin B minor scherzo. My problem was that I hated playing in front of people. I got so nervous, my hands were ice cold and shaking. This applied to all public audiences, obviously, Christine to a degree, my piano professor at the Guildhall, and even Dorian, later to be my husband, who had been a concert pianist at one time in his career. I was so petrified it is a wonder I could find middle C, never mind playing difficult music. With great relief I never play now, but still read music easily.

I supposed that I had better fall in love with her and so I gave up on doing languages at A Level (which I loved) and got a scholarship to the Guildhall School of Music to train to be a concert pianist (which I loathed). Big mistake leaving school early.

I left school feeling sad, lonely and in despair. Where would I ever find other men to have sex with? I was no nearer succeeding in understanding myself. I seriously doubted if I would ever make it with a woman, and felt certain no man would ever like me. This was the first time I wondered if being dead would be a preferable solution. Fortunately, there was always something or someone just on the horizon to stay my hand.

However, the year at the Guildhall was not wasted as I spent some of my grant on going to The Gateway Secretarial Coaching Centre. This was a short motorbike ride away from home, quite near where Lesley lived, and for me was just heaven. I loved Solveig who taught us shorthand and typing. It was hilarious when we had to type to music which she played on an old wind-up gramophone. Inevitably it ran down, with the result that we typed slower and slower. Solveig would suddenly rush over to the gramophone and give it a vigorous wind up, upon which our fingers flew, bells rang and carriages returned with loud crashes. This was in the days of manual machines only. No electric typewriters. I think training in shorthand/typing was the only thing that got me through that horrid year. Needless to say, I much more easily saw myself as a secretary with blood red nails, seamed stockings and vertiginously high heels than I did as a concert pianist in bow tie and tails! I found shorthand fascinating and toyed with the idea of training to be a court reporter. Dad was particularly encouraging about typing and said I'd never regret learning to type – and I haven't.

So – no Guildhall, no Solveig and no money. Now what?

Further Conflict

WONDERFUL to have left the Guildhall and the horror of playing the piano in public. Awful to discover that I had to get a job and start supporting myself. Even with Dad's help I had to start earning and paying my own way. But what? Apart from knowing that I never had to play the piano again unless I wanted to, I hadn't got a clue what I wanted to do. Many years later I realised that this was because I had so little real sense of my self. I didn't feel I was a man even though I was, and I wasn't actually a woman even if I felt I was. I used to look at other men on trains or buses, in the office and in the street, and wonder what it was like to feel that one was a man. At least I had a vague idea of what it was like to feel like a woman. It came as a relief to be told what I was in terms of career and what I should do. At least there was usually someone else – who didn't really know me – more than willing to tell me what I should do.

On the strength of my shorthand/typing I got a job with EMI Records as a filing clerk. It was deadly boring to the nth degree and required absolutely no shorthand or typing. I so wished I was secretary to one of the men. That would have been great – and I would have been good at it, too. The people were lovely – particularly Edna who wore hugely long, floaty leopard-print scarves and called everyone 'Dahling'. I adored her and made a mental note that long floaty scarves were the epitome of fashion. Ann, too, was just my sort of person. She had originally been a model but was now a secretary. She was tall, had a fabulous figure, wore very tight pencil skirts with dangerously high-heeled shoes. She also spent quite as much time showing the other girls how to model clothes as she did answering her boss's phone, typing letters and filing. This entailed teetering up and down the open plan office trailing coats and scarves behind her and doing snazzy little swivelly half-turns on her toes. I was riveted and went straight home to practise for myself. Needless to say, she got the sack because she didn't do any work and her boss got fed up.

This couldn't go on, though. Too boring. What on earth could I do? My first career choice as a ballerina was no longer an option, I felt, so I asked for advice.

'Darling, you've always been so good with people. Why don't you work with people with problems?' from Mum, and 'Get a nursing qualification and you'll never be out of work,' from Dad. Jolly good advice.

So darling trundled off to the local mental hospital, strictly on a month's trial. Miles out in the Surrey countryside saw me riding my motorbike into the depths of nowhere. I discovered that I liked my first three weeks in Warlingham Park Hospital, working on the sick ward for the patients who had physical illnesses as well as a mental illness. Something of a shock, though, when I told the Chief Male Nurse that I would like to train, and found myself on one of the refractory wards.

Oh boy! Here was real mental illness. Patients visibly hallucinating, occasional bouts of violence directed at other patients, the staff, the walls, the windows. Forget nursing – this was custodial care, with a huge universal key which must be carried by all nurses at all times. I was sad that what I thought of as nursing, namely taking temperatures and pulse rates and giving injections, turned out to be managing thirty or more quite disturbed, and frequently strong, men both on and off the ward. However, I actually grew to be fond of my patients and because I was gentle with them I only very occasionally felt threatened.

Once we had passed our first-year exams, we were put straight on nights, which meant being left in charge of one or even two wards by yourself. Returning from three nights off, I was put on one of my favourite wards with mainly elderly people who were generally rather nice, apart from one who hit me very hard on my ear!

Anyway, on this night at about 9 p.m. I did a round to make sure people were in the correct bed and I couldn't find Mr Hayward – a favourite of mine and who, I felt, really liked me. My heart sank. He was in the wrong bed. No. Perhaps he had been moved during my nights off to a side room. No. Not in the loo either. Very puzzling. I went back into the sitting room to discover him sitting in a chair. How could I have missed him.

'Stay where you are, Mr Hayward, while I get a wheelchair and I'll take you to bed. Please don't try to move.'

Back with a wheelchair, but no Mr Hayward. Another round and no sign of him. I decide to go to the nursing office and comb through the previous night nurse's report. No mention of problems with Mr Hayward. Nothing reported for two nights before either. Three nights before, the entry read 'Mr Hayward died this evening.' I was all of a tremble. Sad that Mr Hayward had died while I was away, but also pleased to have seen what I later learned was his spirit form. Dear old Mr Hayward.

Despite having very mixed feelings about mental nursing, once again I loved studying, training and learning new techniques. I was rewarded by getting thee prizes for being top student for each of the three years of my training. Top student nurses were allowed to choose a book for a prize and I chose all three volumes of *The Forsyte Saga* by John Galsworthy – one for each year!

To my surprise, and great pleasure, it turned out that my written work and my ward reports, from the charge nurses who ran the wards I worked on, had earned me the bronze medal as top student for my intake. Nobody qualified for the gold or silver medals that year, although I did know the silver medallist from the year above me. What a lovely man he was and a joy to work with.

Thus it was that I left Warlingham Park Hospital as a qualified nurse, having rather enjoyed 'being' Florence Nightingale – no lamp but a torch for night duty. I found being locked up with insanity for six days of the week too much in the end. The big plus was that I had discovered psychoanalysis, met people in the throes of being analysed and resolved to be analysed myself.

I had just finished reading *The Nun's Story* by Kathryn Hulme, where Sister Luke was a nurse, and *I Leap over the Wall* by Monica Baldwin, a true account of her twenty-eight years as a nun, a canoness regular, and decided that I could escape into the life of a religious – as a nun, preferably. I had been raised in relative poverty and was an obedient kind of person so no problems there. Chastity did present some difficulties. Not to mention that sooner or later Mother Superior would be bound to discover that I had a male body. Sex change? I had by this time discovered that Roberta Cowell hadn't magically become a woman as I, as a child, had imagined. Hormones, surgery and a considerable amount of pain went into it.

Reluctantly I decided against a sex change. I have big bones, size 11 feet and hands to match. How did my parents, who were both small, manage to produce a huge child? Mum claimed it was nine months breast-feeding. I am not keen on unnecessary surgery or the taking of mountains of pills for the rest of my life. One way or another I decided there must be a better way of tackling the rapidly intensifying conflict between Andrew and Andrea, and its attendant episodes of quite destructive bouts of depression.

London Here I Come

CHRISTMAS TIME and the routine visit to see Dad's sister, Elsie, and her husband Bill. I enjoyed seeing my relatives and, in particular, listening to them all talk together. I also really like my cousins, Jeremy who is gay, and Melanie who is now a nun. Also Rashid, Jeremy's boyfriend. I really fancied Rashid and somehow we ended up in a dangerous, but delightful, situation in Auntie Elsie's house that Christmas. Now *that* was a real Christmas present! About fifty or more years later I whispered to Rashid at a party that he had been the first 'man', as opposed to fellow schoolboy, I had had sex with. He choked and had to be revived with a glass of water.

Thank God for dear Jeremy who was living with Rashid in Earls Court. At last some people who took me in their stride, didn't ask questions, and seemed to rather enjoy another member of the family who, to quote Rashid's words, 'was of the same persuasion as us.' On my days off from the hospital I would dash up to London to Jeremy's flat, feeling daringly free. Come the appointed hour, I'd trot off to the two local gay pubs, the Coleherne and the Boltons, on the lookout for a husband and failing that at least some sex. Despite thinking that I was not good looking at all, plenty of older men seemed more than happy to buy me a drink (lemonade shandy in those days!) and to look after other physical desires too.

One evening I met Bill and fell in love with him. He had just come out of prison for being gay and something of a 'chicken chaser'. All my maternal, wifely and nurturing qualities went into overdrive and running a fish and chip shop with him sounded like heaven. He didn't fall in love with me, which was awful as I felt destined to become his 'wife', cook and clean for him and make mad, passionate love with him all night long. Giving Bill his due, he was very responsible. He never said he loved me and made it clear we were ships that pass in the night – or a few nights anyway. This didn't take away the adolescent pain of first unrequited love.

Fifty years later I heard at a group meeting I was at with my husband that Bill had died. While we were waiting at the bus stop to go home I said in a loud voice 'How sad. He was the first man I fell in love with.' Another woman waiting at the bus stop looked a bit shocked and moved a discreet step or two away!

To the enragement of the Chief Male Nurse I left hospital almost as soon as I put my pen down from the final exam paper. How could a top student for three years and a bronze medal winner just leave? I had to get out of the atmosphere of chronic mental illness. We worked six days a week, one of which was for thirteen and a half hours. I dreamt on a number of occasions that I somehow killed my patients by burning the hospital down. The scanty knowledge of psychoanalysis I had acquired during my training indicated that as well as the negative feelings I had towards my patients, I was clearly thoroughly 'burnt out' myself and needed time to recharge my own batteries. Also I wanted my 'Earls Court' evenings available on a daily basis.

However, I had to get a job. Mercifully, Rashid

was an actor and knew of a secretarial agency which was happy to have men on their books. I mounted my trusty, but ancient, schoolboy bicycle and pedalled off to Victoria to try my luck.

St Stephen – Patron Saint of Typists

MRS WHATEVER-HER-NAME-WAS didn't bat an eyelid when I said I wanted some temp work. St Stephen's Secretariat catered for all comers. She pronounced my shorthand 'wonderful', but my typing 'a little slow'. Never mind, it was off to the Civil Service and an all-women typing pool. I loved it. About twenty of us 'girls' sat there pounding on old-fashioned typewriters, typing our knuckles to the bone for all those hunky men – well some of them. The noise level was horrendous. It's a wonder we didn't all end up with a hearing impairment! Mrs Bone, the lady in charge of the typing pool, got a bit of a shock on the first day I arrived when she came to collect me from Reception at the Nature Conservancy in Belgrave Square. Very smart.

'Oh! You're a man. We were expecting a woman.' Don't worry, I thought. In a sense you're getting both in one package.

Mrs Bone always answered the phone to the big cheeses who'd ring down asking for a shorthand writer. As she put the phone down she would say 'Andrew would you go and take down for Mr X.' I always thought that meant something quite different but kept a Sphinx-like composure and went upstairs into the holy of holies, pad in hand and a sheaf of pencils at the ready.

One of my bosses (I worked for four Land Agents) and I shared quite a lot of very intimate details of our lives with each other. He didn't mind at all that I was gay. He even came to bed with me once, but nothing happened. He told me that he had a mistress who used to come to his home some evenings. He would pack his wife off to bed and then have sex with his mistress downstairs. He assured me his wife didn't suspect a thing. What? Either he was delusional, or his wife was too naïve or she decided she didn't mind. Or maybe a combination of all three.

Rush of Guilt

BLAST TELEVISION PROGRAMMES. If I hadn't watched a programme about mental health and seen long corridors peopled with exact replicas of all my patients, I wouldn't have felt so guilty. Here was I enjoying myself for the past year, whilst they probably weren't, and me with qualifications which were supposed to equip me to help them. Lunch hour the very next day and I was on my bike cycling down to Westminster City Hall. Marching in to the Principal Social Worker's office I announced that I had to have a job. With remarkable *sangfroid* Mrs Patterson said 'OK. There's a member of staff on a training course, so there's a vacancy for six months if you would like it.' Guilt assuaged, 'Yes, please.' I was so sad to leave the typing pool, office hours and somehow feeling I was almost myself.

I think I saw myself as a latter-day Octavia Hill or Beatrice Webb with a dash of F. Nightingale thrown in. To say I enjoyed being a psychiatric social worker would not be accurate. A lot of the time I was petrified – particularly on night duty. I really felt desperately inadequate and quite incapable of dealing with a lot of what came my way. My trump card at the time was that I've always been a good listener. Years later I realised that this is often what people really want. And I did agonise over their problems even if I didn't know what to do to help. I was intrigued by some of what I saw, but if I am honest my interest in psychiatry and psychology was purely self-interest.

I needed help and I preferred to be on the staff side of this help rather than on the patient side.

1. Girls together?

2. Anne, Janet and me

3. Dad, Mum and me

4. Janet – with plaits! and Anne

5. Me – without plaits, but with my new tricycle

6. Jolly hockey sticks!

This story, one of the most remarkable in human records, was issued by the Press Association last night

MAN CHANGES INTO WOMAN
Father of 2, fighter pilot

ROBERTA COWELL — a picture taken a month ago of the woman who was once a man, and who IS the father of two children. The change took three years to complete

BOB COWELL, 35-year-old war-time fighter pilot, and the father of two children has changed into a woman

Somerset House has accepted the re-registration, and where was once Robert Marshall Cowell is now Roberta Elizabeth Cowell— an attractive woman with long, golden hair and delicate fingers.

A resident of Croydon, Surrey, he was the son—now the daughter — of Major-General Sir Ernest Cowell, K.B.E., C.B., D.S.O., an honorary surgeon to King George VI and Eisenhower's director of medical services in the North African campaign.

First case?

This amazing change of sex is believed to be the first case in Britain where an adult male has so fully taken on the physical and mental characteristics of a woman. It may well be the most complete change of sex in the medical history of the entire world. Two features help to make it unique:

First, a change of sex from male to female—much rarer than the reverse—has seldom, if ever, taken place so late in life as the mid-thirties.

Second, doctors know of no previous case where such a change has occurred in a man who was already the father of two children.

ROBERT COWELL—a photograph taken in 1939 of the young man who was a racing driver, who became a fighter pilot, a husband and father —and is now the woman in

7. Man changes into Woman
(from the *News Chronicle*)

8. Liz on holiday with me and my family with a wasp up her skirt! Early 1960s

9. Liz putting on a brave face having slipped on seaweed – Mum in the background struggling

10. Betty and me in *The White Horse Inn* – mid-1960s

11. Caroline and Liz

12. Hill School – with Scripture Union badge – 1951

13. Aldy (Alderson) and me in a photo booth

14. Aerial view of Ottershaw School

15. Day out from school – Dad and me punting

16. Chris, my best friend from school, and me in Bath having just left school

17. Christmas on H Ward (where I 'saw' Mr Hayward) – me, the Charge Nurse and John.

18. In the Staff Restaurant with chums –
me far right at the back

19. Getting my Bronze Medal, 1965

20. Is this the right image for London ...?

21. ... or is this better?

22. Typing an OU assessment

23. Off to a Scottish Ball

24. Trixie, me, Gill and Ian

25. Proudly showing off my handwork, my prize-winning cardigan, my beard and my perm

26. Psychology degree from the OU

27. Me, Dorian and Roger Baker – author, gay campaigner, and friend of Dorian's – 1983

28. Ken Livingstone's Partnership Registration – me and Dorian

29. Married at last!

Partners

THE OFFICES of the Mental Health Social Work department of Westminster City Council were housed on the eighth floor of City Hall in Victoria Street. Trixie worked on Reception there and we clicked immediately. By this time I had started learning Scottish dancing and Trixie did this, too.

We both also loved ice skating – even getting to the point where we could dance together, although I fear we may both have looked as though we were driving a bus round the ice rink. Trixie was a very experienced, accomplished and older-than-me woman – especially in the bed department! We actually had sex together quite often, to my amazement, but generally we were more 'girls together' than lovers. We discussed our various men together, one of whom, Bill (a different one) we shared! Talk about confusing. She enjoyed the company of both Andrew and Andrea and found nothing odd about it. She also was a firm believer in reincarnation.

I met Sandy – a delightful, camp American – who became a friend of mine. By this time I was working at Friern Hospital as a psychiatric social worker and occasionally writing for a local gay magazine. Not wishing to write under my own name, in the first issue I called myself Felicity Finger. I didn't like that, so subsequently I became Thelma Thumb! Sandy delighted in announcing from his open top car if we stopped near a bus stop with people waiting 'Look out boys! Here she comes, Thelma Thumb Girl Therapist' which at the time I found very funny and reassuring.

The Thelma bit stuck, but mercifully the Thumb bit was ditched. Some ten years later I was teaching counselling in a social work agency. There some of my students found out about that pen name and called me Thelma, or more affectionately Thel!

From this point on my social calendar became a record of one man after another. I was cruising towards my late 20s and felt a rising panic that I'd never find the right man for me. A stream of rather meaningless sexual encounters left me empty and no nearer my goal – happy husband, happy home. If I really were a woman, I thought, it would be much easier to find a straight man for a husband. Also I would be more attractive as a woman.

I got myself invited to a gay party in Ravenscourt Park one Saturday evening. Barry decided I was 'it' as far as he was concerned. I wasn't sure. I visited the family seat in Cookham Dean and felt thoroughly out of place. Barry had come out to his family years before, but I wasn't comfortable with being outed by association. We were legal by then thanks to Leo Abse's Act in 1967. Barry's mother served asparagus at dinner with the remark to me 'So useful. I don't have to serve a sweet if we have asparagus.' At this point I seriously wondered what on earth I thought I was doing. And when Barry wanted to settle a monthly allowance on me as his 'wife' I made for the exit. He was a sweet, troubled soul, but it felt a bit as though he was trying to buy my constancy and commitment. I have no problem with somebody spending money on me, but for a relationship I wanted it to be based on love not money.

Ron wanted to marry me despite being in a long-term relationship with Bernard. He bought me expensive gifts and could see nothing wrong in my wearing make-up, and even offered advice on using it (having worn it himself when younger). Ron had a sort of faded glamour and worked in the piano department of Harrods. We could have been good 'girlfriends' but I was dead against breaking up his relationship.

Drenched in Miss Dior, hardly able to open my eyes for the amount of mascara I put on, and occasionally wearing colourless nail polish, as a Mental Welfare Officer one of my tasks was to interview people in police custody, escorted by various policemen. How I, too, wasn't arrested remains a mystery to this day. And there were no sniggers either. Amazing.

An eyebrow was raised at home, however,

'*Miss* Dior, darling?' said Mum, picking up some of the bottles on my dressing table. 'That sounds like a woman's perfume.'

'Um, well yes, it is.'

Another gay party in Ravenscourt Park. What is it with Ravenscourt Park? Before I set off I had a hunch I was going to meet a titled gentleman and I did. Heinz's father was the Comte of a town in France, so Heinz was the Vicomte. Heinz was a talented linguist and school teacher, and also very keen on ballet.

I moved into a vacant room in his flat in Chiswick in the anticipation on both our parts that we were 'husband and wife'. The problem was we couldn't decide who was which, so settled much more happily for mother and daughter. Heinz had another 'daughter' who was another of the campest young men I'd yet to meet, with the most beautiful eyes. He didn't live with us.

Heinz had a way of answering his phone with 'Clarence House, Queen Mother speaking,' which I thought an absolute hoot. The only time I tried this it turned out to be his mother, the Comtesse no less, on the other end. Oh dear!

One of the perks of working for Westminster in the Mental Health Department was that we were sent on courses from time to time. On one of these there was a young woman who was full of fun and with a great sense of humour. We became friends and from the outset she knew I was gay and lived with Heinz. On the strength of my modified success with Trixie I asked her to spend the night with me.

Sarah was a delightful girl. I should have known better than ask her to marry me in the hopes that this would settle my problems once and for all. I was going to try and be a man for a change. I grew a beard instead of wearing mascara, met her family and introduced her to mine, who liked her very much. After a holiday with her *en famille*, and after we had broken off our engagement, we found that Sarah was pregnant.

We agonised over this for the few months that early pregnancy allows. We got re-engaged and tried to be happy. Heinz offered to have us live in his flat – baby and all – and I sought endless anonymous sexual encounters with men. Eventually we faced the truth that neither of us would be happy if we got married to each other, so with great sadness we agreed that an abortion would be the appropriate way of spending the money we had saved for our wedding/home.

I heard years later from a student of mine that Sarah was happily married with two children. I was so pleased.

Continuing Conflicts

I MET HARRY IN A SAUNA and he briefly swept me off my feet. By this time I had started the first two years of my training to be a social worker at the LSE. I moved into his flat in Brixton, joined his church choir and tried to be a good 'wife' to him.

For some reason or other he said that he had to invite his boss from the Pru to dinner. Fine by me. Kenneth was very sociable and a trained medium. This immediately re-ignited my recollection of my experience with Mr Hayward and provoked me to ask Kenneth lots of questions about spiritualism, spirit forms and related topics. He suggested I do some reading and directed me to the Psychic Bookshop. I devoured lots of writings, some of which were well-informed and scientific almost in their approach and others which veered towards the sensational. Amusing, but not to be taken seriously.

Kenneth became besotted with me and I eventually left Harry and moved into a small flat in Northwood Hills, relatively near to where Kenneth and Adele (his wife) lived, drawn by my growing interest in spiritualism. Whenever I stayed overnight at their flat, Kenneth and I occupied the marital bed and Adele was shunted off to the spare room. Kenneth and Adele had never had a sexual relationship, whereas Kenneth and I did. It was never discussed, but Adele was not so naïve that she did not wonder what was going on. I wasn't the first young man in their marriage.

Kenneth and I went regularly to the Watford spiritualist church and I saw a number of exceptional mediums working. This was most definitely the belief for me if only because it confirmed my meeting with Mr Hayward on night duty and just made a lot of sense to me. Sometimes Adele came with us.

This *ménage à trois* in which Kenneth and I occupied the marital bed and Adele slept in the spare room was a recipe for misery. We managed to create a living hell, with passive aggression rolling round our trio in a most destructive way. I was fond of Kenneth and also fond of Adele. As a couple they were both fond of each other and Kenneth and I were fond of each other as were Adele and I. It was as a threesome that it was so painful. Both Adele and I broke out with rashes on our hands from stress and Kenneth produced headaches. I discussed the situation with my dear friend Monica, with whom I was working as a social worker in a hospital in Islington. She told me in no uncertain terms to get out of that relationship and get sorted. Boy, was she right. I eventually left Northwood and returned to London.

Developing Circles

KENNETH AND ADELE were marginally interested in reincarnation and we would occasionally discuss this. A friend of ours from the Watford church, Leonora, was also a medium and spoke quite naturally of reincarnation, much as one might talk of elderly relatives. There was one medium in particular I saw at the Watford church called Silvia Popoli. Without any fuss, drama or hesitation she would demonstrate clairvoyance with a confidence and surety that was truly impressive.

I had seen only stage clairvoyance until then, and never as part of a church service. Silvia Popoli was direct and 'no nonsense' in her work. She pointed at people in the congregation saying 'Please answer if I come to you. Thank you.' She then said what she was prompted to say by her spirit guides. She didn't ask for confirmation of what she had said, but moved on to the next person. There were, however, responses which suggested relief, understanding and pleasure and that she was spot on in what she said.

What impressed me was that there was absolutely no suggestion of, for instance, 'I have an Aunt Flossie here with pink knitting. Does this mean anything to anyone?' Well, of course, someone would pop up and say 'I had an aunt who knitted.' Not, for me, very convincing.

I decided to read more about this and discovered that the sort of relationships where one instantly 'clicks' with a new acquaintance can be indicative of a close relationship with that person in a previous incarnation. It can feel like carrying on from where one last left off.

I also came across hypnotic regression, a process whereby a person is induced into a hypnotic state and is 'taken back' many years to previous existences. At first I was a bit sceptical about this until I found out that people who did this could not only describe earlier lives (usually ordinary hum-drum lives) but could also speak the language of that life fluently.

After I had moved out from living with Kenneth and Adele and was again living in London, I decided that I would like to have a private sitting with a medium. As luck would have it, Silvia Popoli lived quite near to where I lived in North London so I booked a sitting with her. The crucial part of her help included telling me that I had had many incarnations before my present one, and that I should seriously consider training as a medium.

Enough other people had suggested this to me so I set about finding a developing circle – the name given to a group of people training to become proficient mediums. Feeling nervous but excited I went for an initial assessment with Maisie Besant, at the end of which she said I could join her circle of between five and seven people.

Each week we met for a couple of hours and learned how to become more sensitive and able to connect both with our guides in the spirit world and with each other. One of the group, Beverley, pointed out to me in a very matter of fact way, over the teapot and steaming kettle, that Maisie had been royalty in some country or other in a previous incarnation! Generally, I was more impressed by revelations of people's previous incarnations if they had lived completely ordinary and unremarkable lives. I am not convinced by people who say they were Cleopatra in a previous incarnation. They are ten a penny, although I suppose *someone* must have been!

A transvestite joined the circle which at the time rather threw me. I wondered why Maisie and her guides addressed this person as 'her' and 'she' when it was fairly obvious he was a man. Now having more insight I can understand and feel comfortable with it.

Give it a Try

RAY WAS A PSYCHIATRIST whose main job was in a large mental hospital in North London, no longer in existence. He did some sessions at the general hospital I was working at in Islington. We became friends and discovered we had a similar sense of humour. One day in the staff restaurant I asked him if he was gay – having a good idea of the answer. He broke out in a sweat and looked really anxious. Even knowing I was gay didn't entirely restore his equanimity.

When his current boyfriend left him, he asked me to be his boyfriend. Reluctantly I agreed, feeling that something was better than nothing. I also felt I had to some extent given up on falling in love with a prospective husband. For both of us I think it was a rather desperate *faute de mieux* leap and after a few months I moved in with him to live together as a gay couple. On the surface I should have been so happy with a very comfortably off, intelligent, amusing man as a partner. But I wasn't. I still hadn't given up on the idea of marrying somebody I was in love with and who was in love with me. I remained on the look-out.

By now I felt thoroughly depressed and hopeless in terms of my life and where it was going. To date I had failed to sustain a relationship with a man beyond eighteen months or two years at the most. Not good. Time to get some professional help.

Freud and Me

IN THE LATE 1960s and early 1970s anybody who was anybody in psychiatric social work was in analysis. Some of my friends were already in analysis and I said to myself that if I hadn't got sorted out and in a good relationship with a man by the time I was 30 then I, too, would find an analyst (and quite a lot of money). I reached 30, still not sorted out, and back at LSE doing the final year of my training to be a qualified social worker. This was much more agreeable and I even quite enjoyed myself! Having filled in all the appropriate forms for the Institute of Psychoanalysis, and been to the obligatory interviews, I was put on a waiting list for analysis. Finally, after six months waiting and using my brilliant fieldwork supervisor as a makeshift therapist, Mr C came into my life.

I first came across Freud during my nursing training and was intrigued by the concept of the unconscious. I'm not sure if I was equally intrigued with Mr C, my analyst, who was what was called 'middle group' – a blend of Freudian and Kleinian approaches. Five mornings a week I lay on his couch and we grappled with my unconscious and slowly changes began to appear. I coped better with anger, my mother, and my patients. However, my dreams and my life generally continued to shout in letters six feet high that I knew I was a woman. How on earth Mr C managed to avoid seeing this I shall never know. Dreaming that I, as a man, went into a Gents public loo and emerged as a woman from the Ladies, seemed glaringly obvious. Apparently my anima was a bit too assertive. It seems that although Freud and Jung split, subsequently middle group analysts didn't dismiss some of Jung's theories. We bickered about this, but in the end Mr C was too clever for me and I decided the least said soonest mended.

Perming my hair, growing my beard and shaving it off more times than I care to remember failed to convince him. He stuck to his guns and whilst I was prepared to compromise by agreeing that I was gay, Mr C continued to say that maybe I needed a female analyst to push me onto the straight and narrow. Possibly, but not yet. It was with some trepidation that I ended my second year with Mr C. This was about the length of time I always broke up with any relationship with a man. He was a good analyst despite being unable to hear my gender confusion. I had done a lot of work with him on my inability to sustain a relationship with a man beyond two years. I felt more relaxed in my sessions and was able to commit to continuing my analysis. I stayed with him for five years and we decided together that I needed a break and possibly a change to a Jungian lady. Curiously he never said a word about my spiritualism or mediumship even when I 'saw' his grandmother standing by his chair and described her in detail.

It was also around this time that I had an out-of-body experience (an OOBE). I woke up one night to discover that I was not in my body which was asleep in bed. I was thrilled as this confirmed for me that spirit forms exist (re: Mr Hayward) and that I was not just my present body. It was a strange feeling re-entering my body which then proceeded to wake up.

In tears I parted from Mr C after five years and sat on my motorbike in Mansfield Road bawling my eyes out. I had learned a lot, was much more stable in myself and had improved as a counsellor no end. The fundamental issue of gender identity remained virtually unchanged.

On the strength of having grown emotionally (and professionally) during my analysis, and possibly because Mr C had at one time worked as a Principal at the Family Welfare Association, I got a job in the Holloway Road office. My role was Student Unit Organiser and counsellor.

I had remained very interested in spiritualism, especially aspects of reincarnation, although I no longer went to any meetings. Having finished going to Maisie Besant's developing circle, I did some reincarnation sittings for friends and colleagues. These consisted of about an hour's session together during which my client was encouraged to sit at ease and I emptied my mind of everyday thoughts as much as one is able. I then waited, eyes shut, until I 'saw', like a film, an episode from a previous incarnation of my client. I would usually have about three of these from different periods. I'd then recount what I had 'seen' to the client and discuss and explain it – or not – according to the client's wishes.

Roger's sitting will remain in my memory for a long time. He was the husband of one of my colleagues and was interested in finding out if any of his previous incarnations were relevant to his current life. Usually two, or occasionally three, previous incarnations were shown to me, the first one being the most relevant. For Roger his first one showed that he had been hanged for some crime way back in the 1700s. This was performed on a crude gibbet and he was just left hanging until dead – and indeed for some time afterwards.

What I didn't know was that he was plagued in his present life by a persistent choking feeling in his throat which was later confirmed by his wife. Following his sitting he no longer experienced this sensation. Fascinating.

Jung and Me

HELEN WAS SENT FROM HEAVEN. She wore dangerously high heels and flicked lovely, long floaty scarves round her neck during our sessions and was a wonderful Jungian analyst. Shades of Edna from EMI Records.

'I'm gay.'

'Wonderful. What are you going to do with it?

Gasp! You mean I haven't got to marry a woman?

Helen, by her own admission, was hopeless on dreams, but she was so good at listening and somehow letting me heal myself. The big difference between my analysis with her and with Mr C was that with Helen I knew I was talking to a warm human being. Mr C was very Freudian and saw the analyst as a mirror. Mirrors can be chilly.

Helen helped me to come out and stop running away from myself quite so hard. We did a lot of good work together and I stopped taking Life quite so seriously and started enjoying myself. At this point I met Dorian, my future husband, who completely swept me off my feet. It could be that at last I'd found the man I'd been looking for and this filled our sessions and may account for my not telling her that for many years I felt I was a woman. I feel sure she would have understood if I had. I can only think that I had given up arguing with analysts about this whilst I was with Mr C and had settled for presenting myself as gay. Also Helen was very positive and upbeat about my being gay.

Open University

AS IF I DIDN'T have enough to do, having psychoanalysis five times a week, whilst I was still living on my own in Hackney I started an Open University course in Psychology. I have always been something of a compulsive student and the OU is excellent. Having completed the first psychology unit, I was so interested that I decided to go for a BA in Psychology. On the strength of my previous qualifications in nursing and social work I was eligible for some credit exemptions. This was a great encouragement to do a full degree.

It was whilst doing this that I had moved in with Ray in our *faute de mieux* move. He had met Mr C briefly in a professional setting and as I was by this time drawing to the end of my analysis with him, Ray felt he could 'see me through the end of my analysis.' Six months later I started with Helen; I left Ray during my time with her.

OU degrees take quite a long time to get, so this was just the beginning of years of study, summer schools, essays and making friends, one of whom I still exchange Christmas cards with.

After my Psychology degree, Eurotunnel happened. I realised we were joined to France, so decided to do a four-year diploma in French with the OU. Finally I did an English degree with them and when I was awarded a degree in Modern Languages and got a First, I then allowed myself to stop all this frenetic studying!

This is It

RUSSELL WAS FOREMOST in the field of the psychiatric aspects of gender re-assignment. He also held regular garden parties in his huge garden for people who were in the process of transitioning, to give them a safe and accepting setting in which to practise socialising in their new gender. He also happened to be a friend of Ray, the psychiatrist with whom I was living at the time.

On the way back from the Chichester Festival Theatre Ray decided that it would be fun to look in on Russell's party. I was not keen, but went along with it. Being still very unsure about my gender I found people who were transitioning both enviable and alarming. However, it being a lovely summer's evening we went out into the garden. 6.30 struck and regardless of where we were and what we were doing, Ray always had to ring his mother at 6.30. He went inside to make the necessary phone call. I went down the fire escape into the garden.

And there was the man I'd been searching for, standing by the wall, smoking a cigarette. Whatever the situation, job, accommodation, friends, lovers, I have always known instantly when the right one comes along. I don't dither, and act on this feeling without hesitating. Dismissing the person he was talking to I asked for a cigarette. (I don't smoke!) I also asked for his phone number, and got it just before Ray returned. I was, by this time, in something of a dither.

Ray, being very perceptive, realised that something had happened. I tried to behave normally and more or less succeeded. The following weekend Ray was on a 'spending the weekend with mother' shift, so I invited Dorian over for lunch. I served a very English salad – lettuce, tomato, beetroot, cucumber and no dressing. Salad cream in a jar if required. Poor Dorian who was used to Mediterranean food and proper continental salads with a French dressing as served by his mother who was Swiss. He ate without complaining, which I now realise was a huge compliment. I braced up and told Ray that I was going to live with Dorian. Very painful for both of us and not a time I would want to live through again.

Despite my feelings of sadness at making do with second best, Ray and I had good times together. We went abroad on holiday twice a year – mostly paid for by Ray – out to meals sometimes and always on a Friday with a child psychiatrist friend of his who was huge fun.

This friend, Don, also had fantasies of being a woman called Jayne. We tended to behave in a rather giggly, schoolgirl way together, pretending to put on lipstick and walking on very high heeled shoes! After I left Ray I heard that Jayne had hanged himself. Very sad.

To my surprise, Ray found a new partner, David, within three weeks and, as far as I know, they are still together. Ray has never been happy living on his own and I was Monty's replacement. Helen, who I was still seeing, commented that Ray had got over me very quickly if a new man was installed so soon. It did make me think.

Four weeks later I moved in with dear Dorian in Osterley. This transformed my life. It's a cliché, but life really did seem to begin (again) for me at 40.

I had always thought I was quite 'out', but compared to Dorian I was still quite 'in the closet'. On our first gay pride march Dorian insisted on holding hands *in front of* a policeman. Not only did I survive, but I felt a great deal better for it. Dorian has always seen partnerships as being about each person enabling the other to grow. He has certainly been that for me.

Permission Granted

ABOUT TEN YEARS AGO, I went on my own to Hurst Green to see my Aunt Sally, who by this time was quite old. Her son Anthony was living with her and was there when I visited. Some people found Anthony a little difficult to get on with, but we found we liked each other's company. In the course of conversation we spoke about his work at a home for boys and young men who had problems living in the community. He invited me to go to Tilehurst one day. I did and found it re-aroused many feelings I thought I'd dealt with. I felt I came across as a total pansy and it was only because I was Anthony's cousin that I was spared any ribald comments. When I shared this with Anthony he asked me why I felt like this.

'I'm too feminine and 'girly' to feel comfortable in the company of all those boys who, I suspect would rag me rotten.'

After further conversation Anthony said that it sounded as though I was transsexual. Coming from him, unsolicited, made an impression on me. We corresponded by letter and this was the start of my feeling encouraged to continue exploring why I felt the way I did. I told him I didn't want to change sex, to which he replied that I didn't have to. At last a member of my family had recognised the difficulties I was having. His acceptance of me helped me to accept myself as different and to look for ways to live comfortably with this.

What I had hoped I had resolved now revealed itself as relatively untouched. The two lives –

Andrew and Andrea – continued to arouse conflict and insecurity in me.

Last Job and Retirement

IT WAS IN 1990 that I started as Principal Counsellor with the Charter Clinic, Chelsea. Prior to that I was working as an HIV and AIDS counsellor for Northwick Park Hospital. There was very little incidence of HIV and AIDS in Harrow at that time and I developed my service to include bereavement counselling. Bereavement, in my opinion, is not an illness – like for instance, depression – and enabling a person to 'bring the dead friend or relative back to life' within their memories, whilst painful, allows them to move on relatively rapidly. I found this area of counselling much more rewarding than working with long-term chronic illness.

I transferred to the Marylebone branch of the Charter Clinic following another meltdown vis-a-vis counselling and therapy. On one occasion when my line manager was reviewing my work with me, I unexpectedly burst into tears. I confided in her that I could no longer find sufficient resources within myself to cope with being surrounded day after day by people with serious mental problems. Within a couple of days she had arranged for me to see the CEO, Patricia, with a view to changing my role in the hospital to a specialist medical secretary.

I gradually cut my hours down after Dorian retired and ended up working three days a week, and somehow accomplishing in those days what I had hitherto taken five days to do. I took early retirement at 63.

The major event in our retirement has been becoming legally married. Having spent many happy years with Dorian, finally I can get to call him husband, although neither of us is entirely used to that yet.

Just Friends

NOW THAT DORIAN AND I were both retired, we joined a social group for mature gay men, called Just Friends. They organised various events, talks, outings and long weekends away which were excellent.

Our president was Donald West, an eminent retired psychiatrist, who had written one of the first academic books for the general reader published in England on the subject of homosexuality. Furthermore, it turned out that he was interested in psychic research. When I heard this I told him that I, too, was very interested in this area. He invited me over to tea so we could have a proper talk about this.

Over tea and biscuits I found myself telling him about Mr Hayward, my training as a medium and my interest in reincarnation. He listened most attentively and said I might be interested in reading a book called *Twenty Cases Suggestive of Reincarnation* by Ian Stevenson MD. I searched around and very soon bought a copy of it.

It is quite a tome, but some of the accounts are very compelling. I read it with great interest and felt quite gratified that my beliefs about reincarnation were largely confirmed. Towards the end of the book it details an account of a child who had died and was reincarnated a few years later into the same family.

At this point the most strange and wonderful thing happened to me.

Revelation

A GREAT STILLNESS overwhelmed me. It was as if I 'saw' a shining golden light caress me from the top of my head and pass right through me to the soles of my feet. As tears filled my eyes I realised that I was in the midst of the most profound experience of my life.

A great feeling of peace and spiritual tranquillity swept right through me. After years of confusion I realised not only who I was, but also why I had lived a life of confusion. I am my mother's dead baby reincarnated, my stillborn sister. This may sound fanciful, but everything now fits together. My mother was a remarkable woman and very wise. No wonder I wanted to be her child.

I am a very impatient person, and without checking properly, I made sure I got reincarnated into my family at the very first opportunity. What I didn't realise was that I was going to be a boy and not a girl. Typically headstrong of me.

The lightness of spirit I felt after my 'reincarnation' discovery was one of the most therapeutic experiences I have ever had. The world slotted into place and my feet touched the ground.

No longer did I have to strive to act like a man. Nor did I have to work so hard to convince people that I was a woman in a man's body. I was free to be me – a gay man in a man's body.

I had never felt confident in the company of men and had always felt I didn't identify with them. In fact I had generally felt rather frightened of men, particularly straight men. Knowing why released a different sort of confidence. I had always felt much more at ease with women and in many instances identified with them quite readily. I now feel relaxed when in social situations and confident to mingle with people – gay, straight, male or female. Now I have got a self that I enjoy, I find that I have a solid self-confidence and this makes a tremendous difference. From childhood if ever I saw a group of boys together I avoided them if at all possible out of fear that they would, almost for certain, tease, bully or attack me. I also continued to feel uneasy in this way with men. Amazingly I now feel relaxed when walking past a group of men, realising that I, too, am a man and can feel part of the group.

For most of my life I wrestled with the belief that I was a woman, Andrea, and at the same time Andrew living in the body of a man. Since I discovered my identity and started writing my story, Andrea has receded into a deep part of my being, and I am happy to be a man no longer in conflict with himself. It is as if I have had two lives – one as a confused man/woman and now, rather late in life, as a comfortable man. I now feel that I am a proper, normal gay man rather than a straight woman making the best of a bad job.

This experience has changed my life in the most fundamental way. For the first seventy-two years of my life I perceived and reacted to the events of my life as the confused Andrea/Andrew person. Now I respond to life events as a solid, self-assured man. Everything in my day-to-day life remains the same, and yet everything is different because I am different in myself.

This has been a strange journey to find myself on, and now that I have done so, I must say that I really rather like 'me'. Obviously this makes me easier to be with, and, interestingly, far less controlling. Dorian has always accepted the strength of my female side, and for this I am eternally grateful. It helps me to believe that others can, too, and on current showing they can.

Epilogue

I THINK IT IS IMPORTANT to say that this is one person's experience of gender dysphoria and how to try to come to terms with it. It is most certainly not in any way a prescription for other people to follow.

For a long time following my conviction that reincarnation is something that we all are part of, I felt that possibly I had been a young Jewish woman who was gassed during the second World War – except that the dates didn't really fit. After I had discovered who I am it made sense of the 'suffocating' element of my feelings since my mother's first baby had been strangled by the umbilical cord during a breech delivery.

In the early 1940s women who suffered still-births were not encouraged to see or interact with their dead baby as they are now. I'm not sure if Mum ever saw her daughter. This may account for her confusion about me and her willingness to go along with my wish to be a girl. As far as I can remember she never quite reached the point of saying 'You're a boy and that is fine. Why does being a girl seem so much better?' Given the status of women at that time, it does seem odd that I wished to be a woman. Janet certainly made it very clear that she thought it outrageous that women were regarded as second-class citizens, as indeed it is.

Although Dad was unfailingly kind and fair to me, I never felt we had a particularly good relationship, and certainly never enjoyed the sort of father/son intimacy that I saw friends of mine having, and that I read about in books. By contrast, Janet and Dad and indeed Anne and Dad had very close relationships, and maybe I thought that if I were a girl I, too, might enjoy this. A weak argument and one that didn't really convince me.

Given my beliefs in reincarnation, and, by extension, a life after the death of the physical body, I have increasingly felt that my relationship with my father has continued to grow since his death when I was twenty-three. I certainly feel that I understand him a great deal better now, which may just be the result of living through the age he was. However, there is also the feeling that he, too, understands that rather curious little boy who teetered round the house in homemade pointe shoes and the red gypsy skirt.

This is a journey that doesn't have an end. Just as I round one corner, lo and behold there is another one waiting for me to explore.

Paradise Press is an independent publishing house, run by a collective within the Gay Authors Workshop. Current titles include fiction, poetry, history and memoirs.

The collective provides editorial and practical support for individual authors publishing through Paradise Press, including a process of collective discussion and review.

www.paradisepress.org.uk

Gay Authors Workshop, founded 1978, is an association of LGBT people who are creative writers – poets, dramatists, fiction and non-fiction writers. We aim to support writers by providing opportunities to meet, to read, to discuss and develop their work.

We hold monthly meetings at different places around London and the South East, but GAW is a national organisation. Our quarterly Newsletter keeps members in touch, while our magazine, *Gazebo,* provides an in-house outlet for members' short stories, articles and poems.

Membership is open to all LGBT writers, from beginners to experienced and published authors. There is a modest annual subscription.

www.gayauthorsworkshop.uk